Color & Garden
VEGETABLES

MONICA WELLINGTON

DOVER PUBLICATIONS
GARDEN CITY, NEW YORK

For Lola and Zoe and Lydia

Note

Many people enjoy gardening, and one of the best things about gardening is that you can plant your own vegetables! In this fun book, you'll meet Lucy and Sam and learn how they create a garden filled with delicious vegetables. Find out what they need, such as gardening tools and seeds, and—of course, sunshine and water! The last page of the book gives you lots of ideas about which vegetables *you* might want to plant, such as beans, lettuce, tomatoes, carrots, and corn. And have your crayons and markers ready, because you can color in every page just as you wish!

Bibliographical Note

Color & Garden VEGETABLES is a new work,
first published by Dover Publications in 2011.

International Standard Book Number

ISBN-13: 978-0-486-47959-0
ISBN-10: 0-486-47959-5

Manufactured in the United States of America
47959512   2023
www.doverpublications.com

Lucy and Sam want to plant a vegetable garden.
They write in their garden journal: People everywhere are starting
to grow vegetables, and today we are going to start, too!

1

In the spring, people plant seeds. Sometimes they plant them indoors, to give them a head start. Sometimes they plant them in greenhouses.

In the city they might plant them in window boxes.
In the country the farmers plant them in big fields.

Lucy and Sam get out the tools they need from their gardening shed.

4

My GARDEN Journal

trowel

weeding fork

Corn

Lettuce

Tomato

seed packets

watering can

spade

gardening gloves

watering hose

hoe

rake

wheelbarrow

shovel

Can you help them find all these tools?

Lucy and Sam get the ground ready for planting.
They have a lot of help from creatures in their garden!

1 Dog

2 Rabbits

3 Birds

4 Snails

5 Ladybugs

6 Worms

Can you find all of these creatures?
Make sure you find the right number of each.

Lucy and Sam plant their vegetable seeds.

Pat, pat them down. Then gently sprinkle them with water.

tomato

peas

carrot

lettuce

onion

radish

Some of their vegetables grow neatly in rows.
Some are not as neat.

Every day their vegetable plants grow taller and bigger and stronger.

Lucy and Sam measure them. They take out weeds.

They water their garden. They make notes in their journal—
their vegetables are growing very well!

tomato   carrot   beet   radish   onion   potato   corn

Some vegetables grow down. Some vegetables grow up.

14

Some vegetables grow around and around.

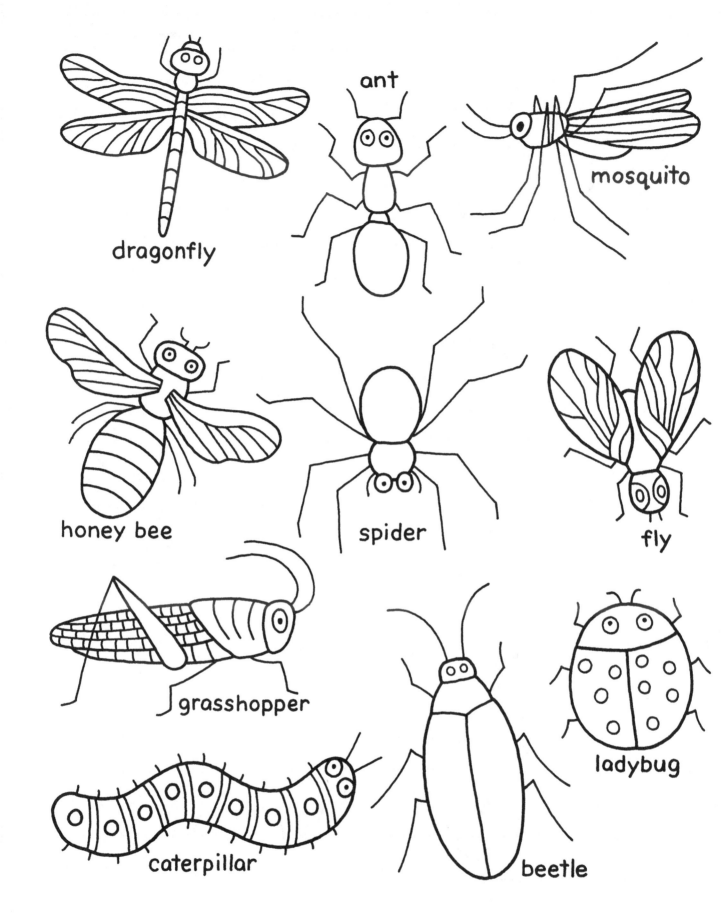

dragonfly

ant

mosquito

honey bee

spider

fly

grasshopper

caterpillar

beetle

ladybug

There are many kinds of bugs living in the garden.
Can you find all 10 of these insects?

Sam picks the first big red ripe tomato.
Lucy pulls up the first big orange carrot.

Lucy and Sam put up a fence so that the rabbits can't eat the
lettuce and carrots. Keep those hungry rabbits out!

Lucy and Sam make a scarecrow in their garden with a wood frame and old clothes. They stuff it with straw. Scare those greedy birds away!

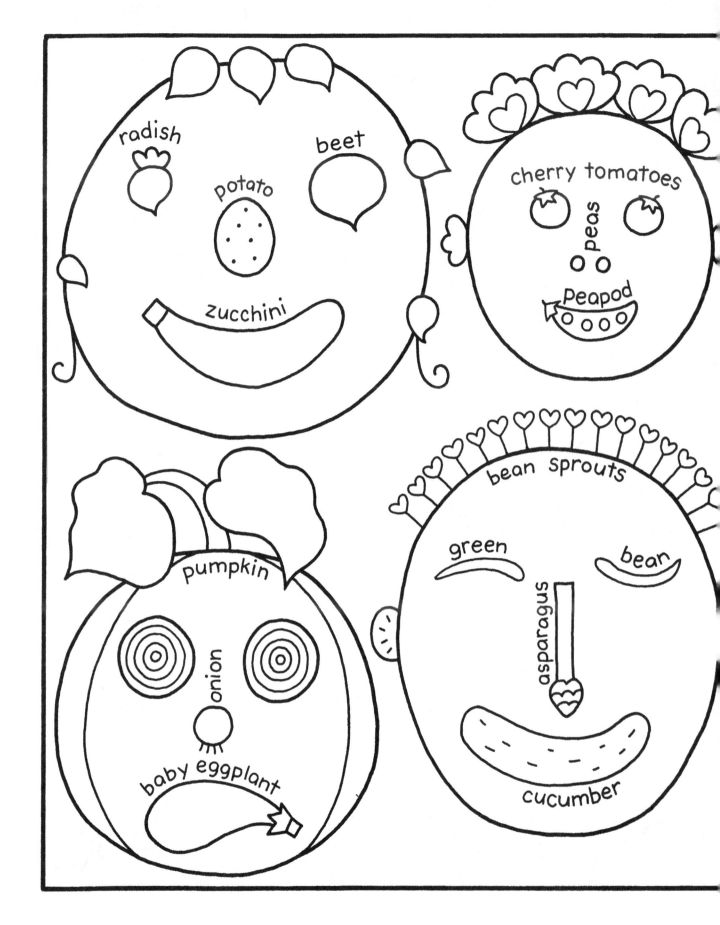

Vegetables come in many shapes and sizes and colors.
They can be arranged to make funny faces!

asparagus
peas
lima beans
tomato
carrot
scallion onion
cherry tomatoes
lettuce
broccoli
onion
corn
cucumber
string bean
pepper
radish

Can you make some funny faces too?

Can you find all the vegetables hidden in this picture?

22

Look for: asparagus, beets, broccoli, brussels sprouts, cauliflower, corn, cucumber, eggplant, lettuce. lima beans, onions, peas, potatoes, pumpkin, peppers, radishes, string beans, squash, tomatoes, and zucchini.

Uncle and Aunt on their farm.
Wish we could visit!

Kitty loves being
out in the garden.

Grandma's spaghetti with
fresh herbs is the best.
Buon appetito!

Lucy and Sam's friends and relatives send them photos of their
vegetable gardens. They paste them into their gardening journal.

Our city friends have a community garden on their block.

Our country friends have a roadside stand.

Vegetable gardens are GREAT!

Our cousin helping in the garden!

Fresh vegetables are growing in so many kinds of gardens:
in the country, in the city, in little pots, and in big fields.

Ripe vegetables are ready to pick. What a harvest! Lucy and Sam are proud.

They cook a delicious soup and make a big fresh salad
with the vegetables from their garden.

Sam and Lucy and their friends love growing vegetables!

Growing Your Own Vegetables

It is best to start with vegetables that are easy to grow, such as beans, lettuce, cucumbers and squashes, tomatoes, radishes, carrots, and corn. Here are a few tips:

- Beans are easy and grow quickly. String beans will be ready to start picking about 60 days after planting. If you keep picking the young beans, more beans will grow, and will continue to grow all summer until the first frost.

- Lettuce grows quickly from seeds—in about 4 to 6 days. It is ready to eat in just a few weeks.

- Radishes also produce plants in 3 to 5 days and are ready to eat in as few as 3 weeks. They can also be planted successfully in pots and grown indoors on a sunny windowsill.

- Tomatoes are a favorite vegetable, but they take longer to grow. It is a good idea to start them indoors. They take 1 to 2 weeks to grow from seeds, and then after a few more weeks they can be planted outdoors when the weather is warmer.

- Cucumbers, zucchini and squash are easy to grow. They usually produce more vegetables than you can possibly eat so they are great to give away as presents! They need plenty of sun, warm weather, and moisture.

- Carrots should be planted outside because they don't transplant well from indoors to outdoors. Replant more carrot seeds every three weeks so you always will have a supply through the summer.

- Corn needs plenty of sun, warm weather, and good soil, as well as more space in the garden than most vegetables. What is more delicious than a sweet ear of corn?

- Follow the directions on the seed packets for the various vegetables. It is fun to keep a record of how your garden is growing in a special Gardening Journal. Enjoy your delicious harvest!

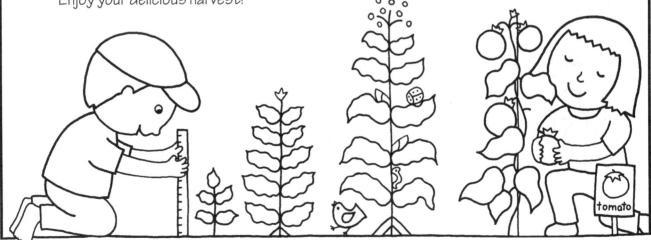

Fun and Educational Books for the Whole Family!

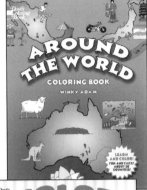

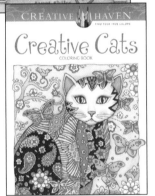

Coloring & Activity Books

Coloring for All Ages & Interests —
Kids to Adults. Puzzles, Mazes, Dot-to-Dots,
Word Play, Spot-the-Differences,
Hidden Pictures, and More!

Arts, Crafts & Hobbies

Papercrafts, Origami, Drawing, Models,
Science Experiments, Music, and More!

Classic Children's Literature

Fairy Tales, Fables, Stories, Rhymes,
and Riddles!

Browse our titles, download FREE sample pages
and activities, or enter a Dover coloring contest.

www.doverpublications.com

 DOVER

*Celebrating 75 Years of Extraordinary Books
at Extraordinary Value*

JOIN LUCY AND SAM IN THE GARDEN

and discover the fun way to eat right and stay healthy with homegrown vegetables. Color pictures of the young farmers as they plant, cultivate, pick, and prepare corn, tomatoes, zucchini, and other nutritious foods. You'll also count worms, protect the crop from hungry bugs, and learn gardening tips that you can use in your own backyard.

$4.99 USA   PRINTED IN THE USA

ISBN-13: 978-0-486-47959-0
ISBN-10: 0-486-47959-5

50499

UPC

8 00759 47959 7

9 780486 479590

Color & Garden
FLOWERS

Color & Cook
PIZZA

Color & Cook
HEALTHY
SNACKS

Color & Cook
BREAKFAST

T2-FAJ-759